K*nown the world over as a breathtaking sight, Crater Lake elicits awe and wonder in even the most well-traveled visitors. The deep blue water, multicolored cliffs studded with evergreen trees, brilliant summer wildflowers or stark white snow—all combine into a tapestry of unforgettable color.*

Fully enclosed by steep walls that rise abruptly from the water, Crater Lake is silent testimony to a volcano's violent past.

Front and back covers: Surrounded by placid blue water, Wizard Island is a riveting sight from the rim of Crater Lake. Inside front cover: Glassy reflections cast by the Phantom Ship give rise to its name. Page 1: The intensely green foliage of mountain hemlock and other trees complements Crater Lake's deep blue hues on a clear summer day. Pages 2/3: Rabbitbrush in bloom adds brilliant yellow to an overlook above Cleetwood Cove during the last days of summer. Pages 4/5: Mount Scott is readily seen across the lake from Discovery Point even in winter. Photos by Jeff Gnass.

Crater Lake National Park, *located in south central Oregon, was established in 1902 to preserve this deep blue lake encircled by multicolored lava walls.*

Edited by Cheri C. Madison.
Book design by K. C. DenDooven.

First Printing, 1996
in pictures - CRATER LAKE: The Continuing Story.
© 1996 KC PUBLICATIONS, INC. •
LC 96-75334. ISBN 0-88714-109-9.

in pictures

Crater Lake

The Continuing Story®

by Stephen R. Mark

Stationed at Crater Lake National Park since 1988, Steve Mark is a National
Park Service historian whose background includes geography and forestry.

photography by Jeff Gnass

Jeff Gnass travels extensively throughout the continent photographing
scenic and historic places, and documenting our heritage lands.

National park areas are special landscapes set aside by acts of Congress to protect and preserve features of national significance that are generally categorized as scenic, scientific, historical, and recreational.

As Americans, we are joint caretakers of these unique places, and we gladly share them with visitors from around the world.

Crater Lake's beauty brings visitors back to it time and time again. A spectacular manifestation of forces which continue to shape the earth, Crater Lake furnishes compelling testimony of how volcanic activity built a mountain and then destroyed it through cataclysmic eruption. Much of what remained collapsed to form a caldera, and then filled with water to become the world's seventh deepest lake. As a model for how such calderas evolve, Crater Lake represents merely a stage in the mountain's development—one which may end abruptly with renewed activity beneath the surface.

Much of Crater Lake's geological story is exposed in cross-section on the inner caldera walls.

A Mountain Built by Fire

Crater Lake is the focal point for the most recent stage of a volcanic cycle that began some 420,000 years ago. This eventually resulted in Mount Mazama, which reached an altitude of roughly 12,000 feet above sea level. It was a high peak in this part of the Cascade Range, part of the larger "Ring of Fire," a chain of explosive volcanoes located along margins of the Pacific Ocean's drainage basin.

A volcano is both an opening in the earth's crust where gas and hot rock are emitted, and a landform resulting from ejected material. Volcanoes in the Cascade Range result from subduction, where moving pieces of the earth's crust called plates override or slip under each other. As the plates move, they trigger earthquakes and volcanic activity. This has taken place for many millions of years over the area now occupied by the Cascade Range. Most high peaks in these mountains are due, however, to relatively recent eruptions well within the past one million years.

A vast coniferous forest covers much of the Cascade Range, but it does not obscure evidence of how stupendous volcanic forces have changed the landscape within the last 100,000 years. Mount McLoughlin and Union Peak are among the many giants seen to the south from Llao Rock.

Successive lava flows separated by airfall debris called tephra help to build volcanoes. Lavas such as these exposed on the Watchman differ by chemical composition and mineral content resulting in a diversity of forms, shapes, and colors. This contributes to Mount Mazama's complex eruptive history, as it does to Mount McLoughlin in the distance.

▲ *The mountain holding Crater Lake retains many of the characteristics of a composite or stratovolcano. This is because many lava flows were interlayered with tephra or other material such as pumice or ash flows. Large cones emerged on Mazama during the mountain-building process, of which Mount Scott at 8,900 feet remains the highest. Much of Mazama was built of overlapping composite cones like Mount Scott which ceased activity long before the climactic eruptions that eventually brought about Crater Lake.*

Grooves cut by glacial ice, called striations, are apparent on rock surfaces at various places around the rim. The striations around the caldera fail to show a regular pattern in orientation. This is further evidence of Mazama being a complex of overlapping cones built by shifting or multiple vents. Wizard Island is a cone formed too late to bear the marks of glacial ice. As the product of post-caldera eruptions, it came into existence about 7,000 years ago. ▽

▲ **G**laciers sculpted Mazama over much of the period during which volcanism built the mountain. While ice carved a noticeable cirque on Mount Scott, it also gouged channels for glaciers to flow from Mazama's summit. The glacial ice advanced and retreated several times, carving canyons in the characteristic U-shape, until roughly 10,000 years ago when the climate warmed. Mazama's collapse some 2,300 years later truncated the glacial valleys, which by that time were largely free of ice. At the head of one such canyon is Sun Notch, over 900 feet above Crater Lake.

▲ *The apparent serenity of caldera walls below*
Llao Rock belies a violent past. After lying dormant
for some 20,000 years while massive glaciers formed
and then disappeared, Mazama awoke less than
200 years before its climactic eruptions obliterated
much of the mountain. Activity at what is now
Llao Rock opened a new crater, which then filled with
enormous quantities of lava that flowed more than
a mile and as much as 1,200 feet thick.

△ **F**ew places along the inner caldera walls possess the geological complexity exhibited on Redcloud Cliff. The sequence of this jumble of volcanic events is still being unraveled by geologists, but the amazing set of exposures has few rivals anywhere in the world. It is unparalleled because Mazama's collapse left evidence of past activity exposed in cross section. Pumice and ash on top of these cliffs are from the climactic eruptions that preceded the collapse.

△ **A**s the final precursor to the climactic eruptions, the Cleetwood lava flow had not yet cooled when the cataclysm struck. Part of this flow oozed back into the caldera once Mazama collapsed.

Mazama ejected so ▷ much material that it represents the world's biggest eruption over the past 10,000 years in terms of volume. Once a stupendous cloud of pumice and ash blanketed a large area north and east of the mountain, so much material had been expelled that collapse became imminent.

Glowing ▷
avalanches called
pyroclastic flows
hurdled down
all sides of Mazama
from new vents
encircling the volcano
just before the
collapse. Those
avalanches choked
all of the mountain's
drainages, including
Annie Creek, where
more than 250 feet
of material
accumulated at
Godfrey Glen.

◁ **As the pyroclastic flows**
continued, they eventually exhausted
the source of buff-colored
pumice. Glassy fragments of dark
gray rock called scoria then
overtopped the pumice and spread
outward, especially on what remained
of Mazama's northern and
eastern flanks. At Wheeler Creek
and in other drainages, seething
gases produced cylindrical vents in
the deposits known as fumaroles.
Heat and chemical action
cemented their walls, making
them resistant to subsequent erosion.
What are called "pinnacles"
became exposed after streams
began downcutting through loosely
bonded material.

15

The Deep Blue Lake

With a maximum depth of 1,932 feet, Crater Lake is the deepest among all lakes in the United States and seventh worldwide. Perhaps this can best be appreciated from the surface, when visitors on the boat tour reach Phantom Ship. At that point they often are told to look toward the top of Dutton Cliff— some 1,900 feet *above* them.

Crater Lake's awe-inspiring blue color results from the interaction of sunlight and water molecules. Other colors of the spectrum are absorbed, but blue penetrates to the greatest depths, especially when a water body has very low concentration of organic matter, suspended particles, or dissolved minerals. In reality colorless, the lake appears blue because those wave lengths are scattered more effectively by water molecules.

America's natural wonders have been set aside and protected for all to enjoy.

Our colorful and informative books are a permanent reminder of the beauty in these special areas.

△ **The relative stability of Crater Lake's water level is due to an equilibrium between input and** output. Precipitation and drainage from springs inside the caldera comprise its input, while the output consists of surface evaporation and seepage. Annual fluctuation in lake level is tied largely to precipitation, especially snowfall which averages 530 inches each year. Correspondingly, Crater Lake will be higher the following summer if more is received.

▲ **Being completely surrounded by water, Wizard Island's conical shape commands the** *attention of everyone at Crater Lake by supplying an immediate and compelling focal point seen from anywhere on the rim. In silhouette, the island appears much like a wizard's hat suspended in midair. From the Watchman visitors can pick out pools and inlets defined by lava flows which lie in relatively shallow water. Were it not for the sparse covering of trees, the eruptions which produced Wizard Island might seem as if they had ceased only decades ago.*

Wizard Island

△ **C**inder cones form from mildly explosive eruptions and are built entirely of tephra or other pyroclastic material. Their symmetrical but steep slopes are topped by a single summit crater. Such cones can also discharge extensive lava flows from vents at their base. Wizard Island provides visitors to Crater Lake with a textbook example of such a feature.

After the Collapse

Covering approximately one square mile of Crater Lake's surface area, Wizard Island began to take shape during the final part of the 300-year period that it took the lake to fill. This island is above several vents in the ring fracture zone, an oval-shaped area of collapse which resulted from Mazama's climactic eruptions. Caving and sliding of walls within this depression widened the caldera, forming a scalloped outline which became its rim. More eruptions produced a central platform on the caldera floor within a century of Mazama's collapse.

Lava flows on top of this platform became the foundation for Wizard Island while the lake began filling. Much of the island formed underwater as Crater Lake rose to a point just 300 feet below its present level. At that point, more than 7,200 years ago, additional volcanic activity prevented the island from being inundated while the lake level continued to rise. It produced rough and blocky lavas from vents located near the water, while also building a steep-sided cone composed of lighter material.

A bleached and gnarled ▷ whitebark pine is among the sentinels which stand silent watch from the top of Wizard Island. This species has experienced heavy mortality near the island's summit crater, where trunks decay slowly in the often cold and windswept conditions. The island possesses a relatively rich flora for such a small and seemingly inhospitable area. Over 100 plant species have been recorded there, a number which represents about one-seventh of the total for the entire park.

◁ *The summit* crater provides deep seclusion to those who climb some 760 feet above the lake. This funnel-shaped feature possesses large and intriguing lava blocks along its lip that sometimes appear in clusters.

The Many Moods of Wizard Island

Wizard ▷
Island leaves an indelible picture in the minds of all who see it. The island seems out of reach from the rim of Crater Lake, very much like in a landscape painting. Distances can be deceptive without figures of a known size near the water.

◁ **Summer** and fall thunderstorms often produce rainbows. Mist and cloud can temporarily obscure the island once heat and moisture bring the release of hail, ice, or rain.

Winter renders Wizard Island inaccessible to all but a group of scientists who periodically monitor
trends in Crater Lake. For one week during this time of year and at several points during the summer
months, they measure physical, chemical, and biological changes in the lake. Despite its seemingly immutable
▽   surface appearance, Crater Lake is a dynamic ecosystem.

▲ *Jagged spires and snow-clad summits impose their presence on many Cascade panoramas.*
Mount Washington, Three-Fingered Jack, Mount Jefferson, and Mount Hood almost form a line north
of the Three Sisters in central Oregon. These peaks are so impressive closer up that land around the base
of each is managed as wilderness.

Amid the Volcanoes

Extending from British Columbia to California, the Cascade Range consists of volcanoes which run roughly parallel to the coast along a north-south axis, dividing Oregon into east and west. Much of the range forms a barrier to moisture-laden clouds. Consequently, the cordillera's western slopes are well-watered and heavily forested, while lands east of the crest become progressively drier until an arid plateau dominates the landscape. This mountain chain's "giants" are seemingly free-standing relative to the lesser landforms around them. Each of the largest peaks is distinctive, in appearance and eruptive history. The only volcanic activity in Oregon during historic times came from Mount Hood in the last century, but its neighbor in Washington, Mount St. Helens, awoke as recently as 1980.

◁ *Some 30 miles south of Crater Lake*
lies Mount McLoughlin, which has a number of
small water bodies below its slopes to reward
the adventurous hiker.

◁ **Mount Shasta is** over 14,000 feet high and towers above everything else in northern California. The mountain consists of many overlapping cones, of which its summit and a secondary feature called Shastina are the most prominent. It can be seen on a clear day from Crater Lake, over 100 miles away.

***T*he right** △ conditions will bring the Three Sisters, 80 miles from Crater Lake, into view. Each of these peaks exceeds 10,000 feet in height.

***M*ount Thielsen's** ▷ heavily glaciated spire is an impressive sight from the rim of Crater Lake. Rising to 9,100 feet above sea level, its summit is known for attracting repeated lightning bolts.

33

Despite the
devastation
resulting from
climactic
eruptions 7,700
years ago, the
forests eventually
returned to what
remained of
Mount Mazama.
High surface
temperatures,
frost heaving, and
a lack of nutrients
in deep pumice
soils worked to
slow recovery of
vegetation near
the rim.

◁ Wind is among
the forces which
shape vegetation
patterns at higher
elevations. Its
prevailing direction is
from the southwest,
and is often
experienced at Skell
Head or Cloud Cap.
Subalpine tree
species such
as mountain hemlock
prefer sheltered
areas, while
whitebark pine favors
more exposure.

△ **A** *showcase stand of ponderosa pine*
can be found along Annie Creek near
the park's south entrance. Its white fir associate
forms much of the understory in this forest
community. The sun-loving ponderosa
can be distinguished by bark which appears
to be pieces of a giant jigsaw puzzle.

W*ater from melting snow can make Vidae Falls* ▷
into an impressive cascade. Located along the
east rim drive not far from Park Headquarters, it is the
waterfall most often seen by visitors. Much of this
area is carpeted with wildflowers during July and August.

Midsummer Bloom

With heavy snows and winter lasting more than half the year, the park's wildflowers have only a short time to bloom. Colors begin to appear in July and proceed up the mountain behind a disappearing snowpack, usually reaching a crescendo by early August. At that point, summer drought and high surface temperatures start to bring an end to the bloom. The season is particularly short at higher elevations, where open slopes resemble arid plains or desert.

▲ **Newberry knotweed and the small purplish** flowers of spreading phlox carpet pumice fields and rocky outcrops near the rim once the snowpack recedes.

Aster fleabane grows beside streams and in other moist places at higher elevations. Blooming from late July until September, it is abundant ▽ near Park Headquarters.

◁ **T**he Pacific red elder fruits during late summer and is common in places along Rim Drive.

Dwarf monkey flower thrives in deep pumice just after the ▽ snowpack's disappearance.

△ *Fruiting heads of the western pasqueflower* appear in July and August once this member of the buttercup family blooms.

△ *Sulphur eriogonum has an umbrella-like* head with persistent yellow flowers that form dense clumps.

△ *Dirty socks is an eriogonum which* grows in the open pumice fields.

△ *Paintbrush is often found* on dry, high-elevation sites.

△ *Woodland pinedrops* are sometimes seen on the forest floor.

◁ *Fragrant subalpine spirea* flowers in July and August.

*◁ **Located at Rim Village, the Sinnott** Memorial Overlook helps to orient visitors to Crater Lake throughout the summer. Rangers give frequent talks on its parapet highlighting the park's geological story. Built to appear as if part of the broader landscape, this structure is almost invisible from the lake's surface roughly 900 feet below. Its designer spent many hours in a boat trying to achieve that effect, something which makes the Sinnott Memorial a masterpiece among rustic buildings. Crater Lake has many examples of this architectural type which prevailed in national parks before World War II.*

***Encircling Crater Lake is a 33-mile road** ▷ called Rim Drive. Open from July to October each year, it allows visitors to stop at a number of observation stations where interpretation is provided through wayside exhibits. As one of the nation's great scenic routes, Rim Drive draws over half of the 500,000 visitors that the park receives each year. This often sinuous road affords superb views of Crater Lake and high points such as Hillman Peak.*

Crater Lake Lodge is the △ park's only hotel. Its season is limited to the summer months because of severe snow conditions at Rim Village. Major structural deficiencies forced its closure in 1989, but a multimillion-dollar reconstruction project followed. In 1995 the lodge reopened, 80 years after the original building welcomed its first guests.

△ **F**ew visitors realize that Crater Lake is among America's oldest national parks. Established in 1902, it predates creation of the National Park Service 14 years later. Led by its first director, Stephen Tyng Mather, the N.P.S. began managing Crater Lake in 1917. Mather's charisma and dedication inspired placement of a commemorative plaque at Rim Village upon his death in 1930.

***B**eginning east of* ▷
Crater Lake Lodge, the route up Garfield Peak is a popular day hike. This trail gains elevation quickly, but allows visitors to see Crater Lake over virtually its entire length.

△ ***T**he golden-mantled ground* *squirrel spends much of the summer caching seeds and can be seen throughout the park.*

◁ ***A**fternoon shadows on the* *Pinnacles can be seen while on a trail above these fossil fumaroles. A footpath connects the park's former east entrance with an overlook on Pinnacles Road.*

Rim Drive is  a popular cross-country ski route in winter. The park has no groomed trails, but many visitors enjoy the wilderness conditions while touring Crater Lake under their own power.

JON GNASS

NPS PHOTO BY ART HATHAWAY

◁ **T**he only way to reach the water is by hiking down the Cleetwood Cove Trail. Once visitors reach the dock, which is about 700 feet below the trailhead, they can take a ranger-led boat tour that leaves several times daily in summer. The tour is the only public access to Wizard Island.

More than 2,000 miles ▷ long, the Pacific Crest National Scenic Trail accesses the high country of Washington, Oregon, and California. It also runs through the park, where hikers can obtain views of Crater Lake from high above Rim Drive.

▲ **Mount Scott is the park's highest point and involves a climb of 2.5 miles from the trailhead on** Rim Drive. Hikers can obtain tremendous views of Crater Lake and the surrounding country from its summit.

Crater Lake Natural History Association

Founded in 1942 to help the park's educational program, the Crater Lake Natural History Association (CLNHA) is a nonprofit organization which also serves Oregon Caves National Monument. It assists the National Park Service by donating funds derived from sales of items in visitor contact stations serving both parks. The association publishes work specific to Crater Lake, for example, the annual *Nature Notes from Crater Lake*. CLNHA also sponsors small research grants (such as rare plant surveys) which directly benefit N.P.S. resource management and interpretive efforts.

SUGGESTED READING

HARRIS, STEPHEN L. *Fire Mountains of the West: The Cascade and Mono Lake Volcanoes*. Missoula, Montana: Mountain Press Publishing Co., 1988.

NELSON, C. HANS, ET AL. "The volcanic, sedimentologic, and paleolimnologic history of the Crater Lake caldera floor, Oregon: Evidence for small caldera evolution." *Geological Society of America Bulletin*, 106, (May 1994), 684-704.

SCHAFFER, JEFFREY P. *Crater Lake National Park and Vicinity*. Berkeley, California: Wilderness Press, 1983.

WARFIELD, RONALD G., LEE JUILLERAT, and LARRY SMITH. *Crater Lake: The Story Behind the Scenery*. Las Vegas, Nevada: KC Publications, 1982.

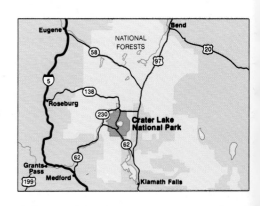

UMPQUA NATIONAL FOREST

230

138

WINEMA
NATIONAL
FOREST

North
Summit Rock

0   1   2 Kilometers
0   1   2 Miles

Pacific Crest Trail

Other hiking trail

Ranger station

Picnic area

Campground

Gasoline

North Entrance Station

DESERT RIDGE

Boundary Springs

Bald Crater

Desert Cone

PUMICE
DESERT

Oasis Butte

Sphagnum Bog

Red Cone

Grouse

Cleetwood Cove Trail

Llao Rock

CLEETWOOD
COVE

Rim Drive
(closed in winter)

Wineglass

Sharp Peaks

Bear Butte

Scout Hill

Rogue River

Devil's Backbone

Rim Drive
(closed in winter)

The
Watchman

WIZARD
ISLAND

CRATER
LAKE

Maximum lake depth:
589 meters
1932 feet

Skell
Head

Pumice
Castle

Cloudcap

Castle
Rock

Mount Scott
2721 meters

Lightning
Spring

Discovery Point

Lake surface elevation:
1882 meters
6176 feet

Phantom
Ship Overlook

Pacific

Crest

Trail

Bybee

Creek

Rim Village Visitor Center
Sinnott Memorial Overlook

Cafeteria
Rim Center

Crater Lake Lodge

Phantom Ship

Dutton
Cliff

Sun Notch

62

Visitor
Information

Steel Information Center

Park Headquarters

Castle Crest
Wildflower Trail

Rim
Drive
(closed in winter)

Vidae Creek

Thousand
Springs

Castle Point

Watchman Point

Annie Spring
Entrance Station

Annie Spring

Grayback Road
one way

RIVER
NAL
ST

Huckleberry Mountain

BacTop Butte

Mazama Village

Godfrey Glen Trail

Annie Spring
Canyon Trail

Arant Point

Duwee Falls

THE PINNACLES

Union Peak

Scoria Cone

Maks Crater

PUMICE
FLAT

Bald Top

Stuart Falls

Goose Nest

WINEMA

232

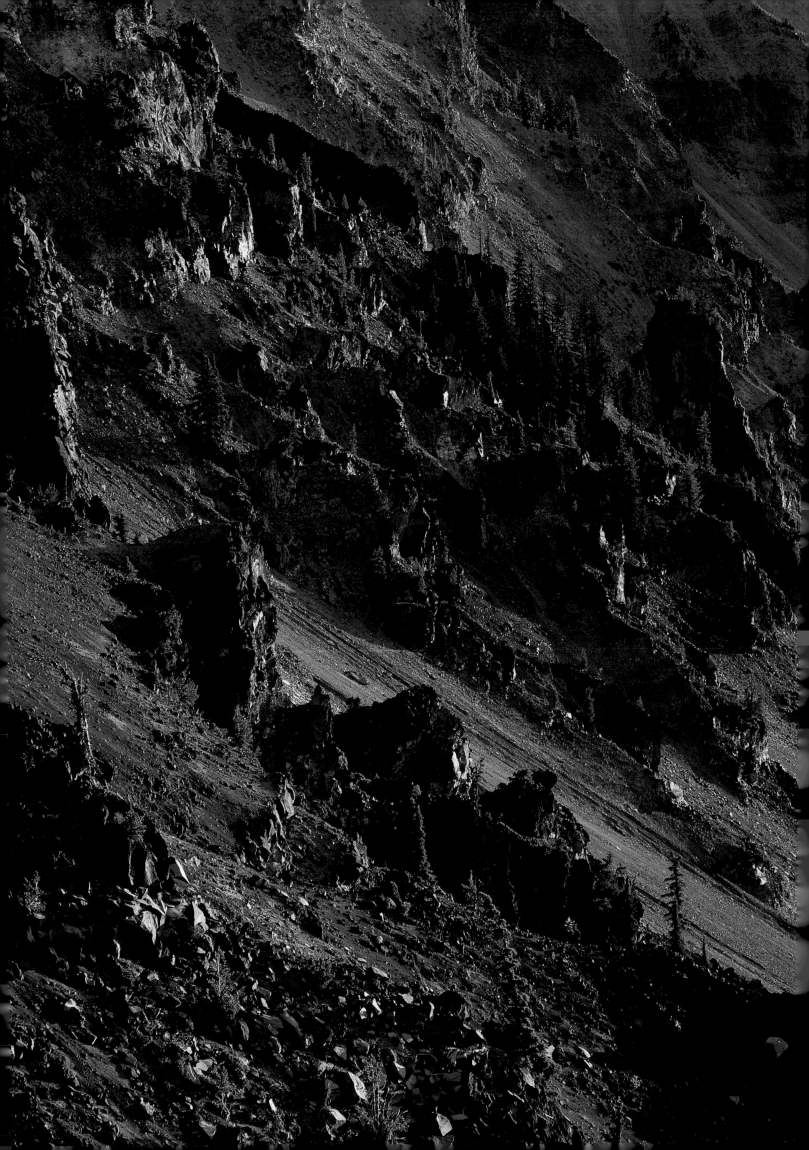

What we see as Crater Lake represents just a moment in geological time. The apparent serenity of rock, water, and forest may one day be shattered by a reawakening of Mount Mazama. This would herald a new chapter in the volcano's history, one which could greatly alter what is often accepted as the unchanging face of Crater Lake. Renewed activity is a frightening prospect, but one that might not come for centuries. Until then, the caldera and its surroundings will continue to awe and inspire visitors. Some of them are enthralled by reflections in the water on a clear day or the compelling form of Wizard Island. Others view Crater Lake in larger context, as an unusually clear example of how great eruptive forces can shape the earth's surface and give rise to an incomparable lake. Regardless of how well they understand the forces that created and continue to affect Crater Lake, the majority of visitors find themselves wanting to return again and again.

Largely resistant to erosion, volcanic dikes such as the Devil's Backbone lie exposed on the caldera's walls.

▲ ***Although Crater Lake represents a monument to uncertainty, it is also a supreme expression of*** *beauty. Photographers have flocked to the lake for more than a century, each one eager to capture the caldera's sublime colors. At sunset, Crater Lake seems especially quiet and fathomless, a primitive landscape in the fast-fading light.*

Books on national park areas in "The Story Behind the Scenery" series are: Acadia, Alcatraz Island, Arches, Big Bend, Biscayne, Blue Ridge Parkway, Bryce Canyon, Canyon de Chelly, Canyonlands, Cape Cod, Capitol Reef, Channel Islands, Civil War Parks, Colonial, Crater Lake, Death Valley, Denali, Devils Tower, Dinosaur, Everglades, Fort Clatsop, Gettysburg, Glacier, Glen Canyon-Lake Powell, Grand Canyon, Grand Canyon-North Rim, Grand Teton, Great Basin, Great Smoky Mountains, Haleakala, Hawaii Volcanoes, Independence, Lake Mead-Hoover Dam, Lassen Volcanic, Lincoln Parks, Mammoth Cave, Mesa Verde, Mount Rainier, Mount Rushmore, National Park Service, National Seashores, North Cascades, Olympic, Petrified Forest, Redwood, Rocky Mountain, Scotty's Castle, Sequoia & Kings Canyon, Shenandoah, Statue of Liberty, Theodore Roosevelt, Virgin Islands, Yellowstone, Yosemite, Zion.

Additional books in "The Story Behind the Scenery" series are: Annapolis, Big Sur, California Gold Country, California Trail, Colorado Plateau, Columbia River Gorge, Fire: A Force of Nature, Grand Circle Adventure, John Wesley Powell, Kauai, Lake Tahoe, Las Vegas, Lewis & Clark, Monument Valley, Mormon Temple Square, Mormon Trail, Mount St. Helens, Nevada's Red Rock Canyon, Nevada's Valley of Fire, Oregon Trail, Oregon Trail Center, Santa Catalina, Santa Fe Trail, Sharks, Sonoran Desert, U.S. Virgin Islands, Water: A Gift of Nature, Whales.

A companion series of national park areas is the NEW "in pictures...The Continuing Story." This series has **Translation Packages**, providing each title with a complete text both in English and, individually, a second language, German, French, or Japanese. Selected titles in both this series and our other books are available in up to five additional languages. **Call (800-626-9673), fax (702-433-3420), or write to the address below.**

Published by KC Publications, 3245 E. Patrick Ln., Suite A, Las Vegas, NV 89120.

***I**nside back cover:* ▷
Phantom Ship is often hard to distinguish from the lake and nearby cliffs. Photo by Jeff Gnass.

Created, Designed and Published in the U.S.A.
Printed by Dong-A Publishing and Printing, Seoul, Korea
Color Separations by Kedia/Kwangyangsa Co., Ltd.